For _____
From Trevor S.

SCHOLASTIC

Tangled in Beauty:
Contemplative Nature Poems

Poems by
Isabel Joy Kim & Siona Prasad

Art and Photography by
Isabel Joy Kim

Philokalos Press Vienna, Virginia

Copyright © 2013 by Isabel Joy Kim and Siona Prasad
All rights reserved
Printed in the United States of America

Library of Congress Control Number: 2013922740
ISBN: 978-0-9912472-0-2

10 9 8 7 6 5 4 3 2

Cover Graphic Design: Kavin Lee
Cover Painting: "Seasons" by Isabel Joy Kim
All photographs printed in this book were taken by
Isabel Joy Kim with her hand-me-down Nikon D70s
camera (thanks to cinematographer Adam McDaid)

Mailing Address:
Philokalos Press, LLC
P.O. Box 3811
McLean, VA 22103
www.philokalospress.org

For all the dreamers ...

Dreams

A song sweeping into my sleep,

a melody beyond human reach,

a distant world ready to be found,

where passion is so deep,

where love is rightly crowned.

-Isabel Joy Kim

table of contents

~ winter ~

lament	isabel & siona	11
a winter night	isabel	13
winter ice	siona	14
first snowfall	siona	16
the grey monolith	isabel	17
moon	siona	18
owls	isabel	19
winter	isabel	20

~ spring ~

clouds	isabel & siona	23
infant	isabel	24
thaw	isabel	25
river	isabel	28
lotus	siona	29
magnolia	isabel	30
a green lily pad	siona	31
far away green	isabel	33
reflection	isabel	35

~ summer ~

the mare	isabel & siona	39
the stallion	siona	41
mowers	isabel	42
hurricane	isabel	43
the sun	siona	44
mother	isabel	45
history lesson	siona	47
Fourth of July	siona	48
secrets	isabel	49
the beach	siona	51
stars	isabel	52
sunset	siona	53

~ fall ~

in the apple orchard	isabel & siona	57
goodbye	siona	58
pebbles	isabel	59
fall again	isabel	61
autumn	isabel	62
kittens	isabel	64
autumn leaves	siona	65
whisper	isabel	67
dusk	siona	68

acknowledgements 70

about the authors 71

~ winter ~

lament

a silver bell sings
a sorrowful tune
a chimney swallow rustles
from her perch in the mist
then flees.

isabel & siona

a winter night

the trees are swaying within the wind,
there's a blanket of snow on the ground,
the skies are darkening, the air is thickening,
the sun is starting to fall,

> you can barely see the stars
> shining in the sky,
> these are all the signs
> of a winter night

the foxes are scurrying to their dens
where their warm havens lie,
the birds are rustling, the plants are bending,
the moon is starting to rise,

> you can barely see the stars
> shining in the sky,
> these are all the signs
> of a winter night.

isabel

winter ice

the barren trees shudder
the wind whispers the sounds of our past
the fallen leaves rustle in their grief
our tears fall down, and the earth swallows them
the angry air whips at the thin line connecting us
the dark clouds thunder, the air turns to ice
and shatters what's left of us.

siona

first snowfall

the clouds grow grey, the winds blow strong
the snow dusted trees wave arms so long
a thin, white blanket covers the ground
delicate snowflakes fall with no sound
the first snow of the season is finally here
everyone, anywhere, give a big cheer

my fingers are numb, and so are my toes
I jump into a big white pile of snow
my eyes water, my nose is red
I want to snuggle up in my bed
we make a snowman, I and my peers
I hope my snowman doesn't disappear

much to my teachers' dismay
we don't have any school today
I skate for hours, ski like a pro
I have a great time in our first snow
I have played all day with no sight of the sun
I wish I didn't have to leave all this fun.

siona

the grey monolith

so many suns
lived

the grey
monolith

formed by the
wind

covered in white
snow.

isabel

moon

shining in darkness
a white mirror in heaven
floating in crisp air.

siona

owls

eyes like blue diamonds,
peering through your hidden soul,
revealing secrets.

isabel

winter

in the evergreens,
when winter springs,
enchantment engulfs almost everything

the endangered come out of hiding,
entering a world
of enduring wonder

snow ever dusting the leaves,
blessing the canopy of trees.

isabel

~ spring ~

clouds

nature's tearful mists
wisps of white flying through blue
tangled in beauty.

isabel & siona

infant

a lovely creature,
chubby and small,
cuddly and cute,
too little to walk,
too delicate to fall.

isabel

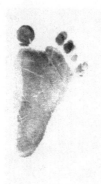

thaw

I feel the wind dance around my fingers,
an ant wiggle atop my toe,
the rush of water beneath my feet,
escaping the melting snow

the rays of sunlight from above
cast shadows upon the cold,
and the flowers frozen in crystal
reach out to the coming warmth.

isabel

river

run,
flow,
run,
and know,
you're a shimmering serpent,
a melted pearl,
a twirling wind,
embracing the world.

isabel

lotus

her light pink petals are streaked with magenta
she blossoms to the sun
asking for blessings
beneath her flows cooling water
mesmerized by her delicate touch
the long green grasses bow down
the white clouds move across the pond
the mountains rise
as the lotus flower awakens
to the sun's golden rays.

siona

magnolia

bloom,
grow,
a speck of pure snow,
a blossom of honey
and sunlight,
petals of nature's velvet,
a wondrous aroma
of life.

isabel

a green lily pad

there is so much more
to

a green
lily pad

sitting on the rippling
waters

singing to the
frogs.

siona

far away green

green grows in places you know,
like gardens, and greenhouses too,
but green also grows in a place called heaven,
that's how far green can go.

isabel

reflection

water blends with the sky,
a dew drop falls off
a leaf and sends a ripple
across the sky.
a heron sits on the surface
of the water, the horizon
of above, then looks
to her blue surroundings
and sighs.

isabel

~ summer ~

the mare

when she runs,
her hair blows behind her like wisps of smoke,
each beat of her hooves is a heartbeat of the earth,
each breath she takes makes the air tremble,
each blade of grass below her bends with respect,
each blink of her eye opens doors to new life,
each swish of her tail spreads love and passion,
the mare.

isabel & siona

the stallion

ominous clouds streak the sky
the air quivers with tension
my feet are pins and needles
I strain to see the track
then I see him,
his head thrown high
his silk coat gleaming
his large eyes darting from side to side
he knows what he is here for
he kicks his front legs and rears high into the air
as the stallions enter the starting gates.

siona

mowers

grassy hills of grace,
making fields of lace,
growing swiftly until
the mowers come to stay.

isabel

hurricane

like a mother wind walking through a vast valley
of little grasses,
she makes the grasses rustle,
she makes them bend,
she makes them bow down to her,
she knows she is the hurricane.

isabel

the sun

she is like ...
the warmth of a hug
the blanket that keeps you snug
the peace in a war
the queen of the outdoors
the courage that fights the darkness
the hope in the deepest abyss.

siona

mother

a mother's warmth is like sunshine
warming you from the inside,
sweet love pushing through
the bitterness that lives within,
so hug your mother closer than the air,
for love is warm sunshine.

isabel

history lesson

ahead of me lies a barren field
scarred with sweat
and darkened by sin

their backs are bent
their voices are hollow
but their master sits content

he smokes his pipe
under the shady tree
and the honey just drips around him

they yearn for the western sky
where the birds play and soar
and the free eagle makes its daily rounds

their hearts fill their entire chest
loyalty in their actions
though their eyes say something else

on this hallowed ground, aching heavy in the air,
their message rolls in the waves of the sea,
carried in every droplet of despair

we who have a heart
who know love as a prize
must see this thirst for freedom
in their very eyes.

siona

Fourth of July

the night is black with hints of gray
the stars peek through their windows of light
our flags wave high
above the trees
above the clouds
above our flying souls
for it is the Fourth of July.

siona

secrets

I have never found the secrets
to the sky and seas, all the keys
to the secret doors, they flee,
the wonders of the sky are just
out of my reach, and the seas
are far too deep.

isabel

the beach

the rise and fall of the waves
calling me
the sound of the ocean
rushing through my ears
the sky a swirl of red and orange
blinding me
the soft sand falling through my fingers
sparkling like crystals
reflecting light in every direction
the salty taste of water on my tongue
as I somersault into the coming wave
a summer to remember.

siona

stars

the laughter of the stars can be heard,
high above the wondrous seas,
they dance with the melody of the moon,
and bask in the delight of the sun,
and even the smallest grain of sand can hear
the laughter of the stars.

isabel

sunset

embraced in her warmth
flames dancing on the blue waves
bathing Earth in light

siona

~ fall ~

in the apple orchard

the busy ants scurry up a hillside
a pair of ladybugs flutters onto a leaf
the grass moves to the pulse of the wind
as two squirrels weave through the apple trees

we see the sky fade behind the falling leaves
the warm apple cider leaves our thoughts dry
our song is sung by two cardinals in the distance
the pumpkins lay scattered on the ground

the crisp air makes us huddle together
but the silence makes us hold our breaths.

isabel & siona

goodbye

I stand between two mountains
ahead of me the sun shines
but dark clouds shadow my past
I can still hear the echoes of our last goodbyes
they leave my thoughts bitter
a gust of wind pushes me forward
I trip and fall
I turn back and stare at the rain
I cannot say goodbye.

siona

pebbles

the pebbles look to the sky,
there,
they spy
droplets of rain,
birds in the air,
the trees, they sway —
the pebbles lay,
and yet they pray.

isabel

Fall again

the sun sets softly in the distance
as it touches the ground
its rays shoot across the earth
and everything green turns red and orange
spirits awaken and memories come to life
it is Fall again

siona

autumn

the leaves fall,
like a sunset
in the spring,

a bird dancing beneath
growing clouds,

a soft lamb prancing
in a field,

the wind,
carrying them farther.

isabel

kittens

their fur is a tuft of feathers,
whiskers, like swirls of smoke,
their eyes as large as the moon,
more mystifying than a ghost.

isabel

autumn leaves

the sky a swirl of falling leaves
drifting with the wind in an autumn dream
wings of beauty flying high
whirling around us as heaven's eye
the leaves dance to the tune of our hearts
whispering with passion, nature's art

siona

whisper

the amber sky is up again,
the air becomes intense with silence,
only the whisper of the rolling waves can be heard,
    rise,
fall,
    drift,
call,
the wind is quiet and listens to its whispering
neighbor,
the sea.

isabel

dusk

the wind blows through my hair
the song of the sparrow fills the air
the afternoon sky is a darkening blue
with wisps of white swirling through
the evergreen trees sway in the breeze
looking up at the sun
through their fluttering leaves
Nature has her own shining armor
and glittering knife,
guiding you through the obstacles
and to the beauty in life.

siona

acknowledgements

Isabel Joy Kim would like to express her deep gratitude to: Dr. Suzanna Henshon, for her encouraging feedback; my teachers, past and present, for their rigor as much as their encouragement; my friends, who bring sanity and laughter to my day; my loving halmonis and harabujis, Grace, Victor, Sue, Harry, Jung-nim and Keum-soon; my thoughtful aunties and uncles, Juna, Dan, Petey, Michelle, James, Ann, Mike and Danny (wish I could have met you); Daddy, Eugene, for instilling in me a love of reading; Mommy, Jumi, for sharing her love of learning with me and encouraging me to never give up; my sisters, Emilia and Elinor, best friends for life; and my co-dreamer, Siona, how can I thank you for the gift of our friendship?

Siona Prasad would like to express her heartfelt thanks to: Dr. Henshon, for her feedback and support of our project; our publisher, Jumi Kim, for her thoughtful comments, especially during revising and editing; my teachers, for the pure love of learning they have instilled in me; my friends, for adding a touch of imagination and endless possibility to my day; my loving grandparents, Dadagi Rati and Nanigi Nirmala; my brother, Neeraj, who is probably too busy with biology to read this; Daddy, Kuldeep, for keeping me laughing all the time; Mum, Seema, for her undying support; and my co-dreamer, Isabel, for your constant friendship and support (don't stop running around with your eyes closed!)

about the authors

Isabel Joy Kim is co-author and illustrator of *Tangled in Beauty: Contemplative Nature Poems*, her first published book. Isabel is a 7th grade honors student in the Advanced Academics Program of Fairfax County Public Schools and lives in northern Virginia with her parents, two sisters and two cats. In 2009, Isabel was the runner-up winner of the National Zoo's Poster Contest. In her scant spare time, Isabel enjoys music, nature hikes, and reading a little J.R.R. Tolkien every night with her family.

Siona Prasad is co-author of *Tangled in Beauty: Contemplative Nature Poems*, her first published book. Siona is a 7th grade honors student in the Advanced Academics Program of Fairfax County Public Schools and lives in northern Virginia with her parents, brother and grandfather. Recently, Siona's First Lego League Team "Positive Aftermath" won the 1st Place Grand Champions Award at the VADC Championship Tournament. She is a rare example of the implausibly left-brained poet.

"If I read a book and it makes my whole body so cold no fire can warm me, I know that is poetry. If I feel physically as if the top of my head were taken off, I know that is poetry. These are the only ways I know it. Is there any other way?"
— Emily Dickinson, *Selected Letters*

If you enjoyed this book of poems (and feel even a smidgen of what Emily Dickinson describes above), the book's authors would love to hear your **positive review**, on or offline, and would be grateful for your help in **spreading the word** about their book! They may be reached at: **info@philokalospress.org**.

If you are interested in receiving periodical news updates from the publisher concerning book launch events, author interviews, media appearances or pre-release specials, please sign up for Philokalos Press's newsletter at: **www.philokalospress.org/news.html**

Thank you for your support of Philokalos Press!

Made in the USA
San Bernardino, CA
02 April 2014